W9-BXN-688

# Let's Play Tag!

📖 Read the Page

▶ Read the Story

🔁 Repeat

⬛ Stop

⭐ Game

Level 1    Level 2    Level 3

TO USE THIS BOOK WITH THE TAG™ READER you must download audio from the LeapFrog Connect application. The LeapFrog Connect application can be installed from the CD provided with your Tag Reader or at leapfrog.com/tag.

# Tractor Tipping

It was nighttime in Radiator Springs. The tractors were asleep in the field. Mater was taking his friend Lightning McQueen out for a night of tractor tipping.

"You'll love it. Tractor tipping's fun," Mater said. "But don't let Frank catch you."

"Wait. Who's Frank?" McQueen asked as he followed Mater down the hill.

 "Okay, here's what you do," Mater said.

"You just sneak up in front of 'em ..."

"... and then ..."

**HONK!**

The tractor snapped awake and fell over
with a loud **MOO!**

**KER-THUD!**

"I tell you what, buddy—it don't get much better than this," Mater laughed.

"Yep, you're living the dream, Mater boy," McQueen replied.

But McQueen was only teasing Mater. He thought tractor tipping was silly.

"Your turn," Mater said.

McQueen didn't want to do it.

After all, he didn't have a horn!

"Chicken! Bwawk! Bwawk!"
Mater teased.

McQueen was no chicken.
He was a famous race car!
He could handle anything!

So McQueen snuck up on
a sleeping tractor and ...

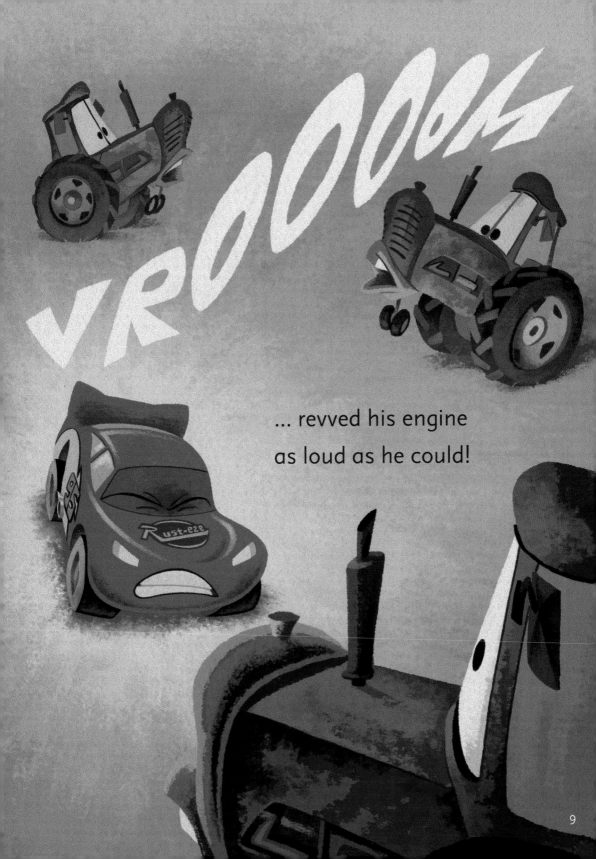

VROOOOOM

... revved his engine
as loud as he could!

McQueen's engine was so loud, it woke up ALL the tractors.

KER-THUD!

KER-CHUNK!

And made them ALL tip over!

KER-BONK!

Mater and McQueen laughed.

This was the greatest tractor tipping
night ever!

Suddenly, they heard a **ROAR!**

"That's Frank!" Mater shouted as he
zipped away.

Frank was a giant combine, the
biggest McQueen had ever seen.

And Frank looked angry!

Mater and McQueen had to get away fast. ZOOM! Together, they headed for an opening in the fence. As they sped off, Mater laughed out loud.

"Run! Frank's gonna get you!" he teased.

McQueen didn't laugh at Mater's joke.
He just raced faster than he had ever
raced before.

McQueen and Mater zoomed through the broken fence. But Frank was so big, he couldn't fit through the opening to chase them.

It was a safe getaway for Mater and McQueen!

"You gotta admit, that was fun!"
Mater said.

"Oh yeah," McQueen replied.

Tractor tipping sure was a strange way to
spend an evening, but McQueen knew
this was one night he'd never forget.

tag ten beg van
bag tan bed mad

Customers!

WELCOME
TO RADIATOR SPRINGS

e

n

d

whiz

wheel

when

shine

shop

show

**Pulling Bessie!**

ch

sh

th

thunder

third

chain

thank

charm

chase

21

roadmap

toolbox

taillight

pothole

stop

tool

flag

pot

tail

fire

road

*Tow Mater!*

 tow cable

grille

exhaust pipes

fender

spoiler

nozzle

supercharger

hydraulics

lifting fork

whitewall tire

Mack

Guido

Ramone

*Car Parade!*

Red

Snot Rod

Wingo

Flo

Lizzie

Mater

25